# Shamanic Wisdom for a Shifting World

Compiled and Edited
by
Nancy Wastcoat M.Ed. and
Michael J Garbett Ed.D.

Copyright © 2016 by WiseGuides, Inc.

Section comments and Photography by Nancy Wastcoat
Cover design and book design by Michael Garbett

All rights reserved.

No part of this book may be reproduced, scanned, or distributed in any form or by any electronic or mechanical means including information storage and retrieval systems, without permission in writing from the authors. The only exception is by a reviewer, who may quote short excerpts in a review.

Printed in the United States of America

First Printing: August 2016

ISBN 978-0-9977633-0-0

# Dedication

*To those who seek a richer and more complete life.*

# Table of Contents

| | |
|---|---|
| Why We Are Writing This Book | 5 |
| Wisdom Keepers | 9 |
| What is Shamanism? | 12 |
| Who are Shamans? What Roles Do They Play? | 16 |
| Why Shamanism Now? | 20 |
| Shamanic Cosmology | 25 |
| Shamanism and Connectedness | 30 |
| Levels of Engagement | 36 |
| Maps of Consciousness | 40 |
| What is Energy? | 44 |
| What is Fear? | 48 |
| What is Healing? | 50 |
| Creating Reality | 58 |
| Evolving Consciousness | 61 |
| Religion and Shamanism | 65 |
| Spirituality and Shamanism | 69 |
| Business and Shamanism | 72 |
| Government and Shamanism | 77 |
| Shamanism and Modern Culture | 80 |
| Shaman's Messages to the World | 82 |

# Why We Are Writing This Book

For the past nineteen years, we have had the good fortune to work, study, and travel with many Peruvian healers, anthropologists, and archeologists. Because of them, our life has become richer.

This may, at first, come as a surprise. Life in Peruvian villages, deserts, jungles and high mountains appears simple and, perhaps, impoverished by some standards.

More a feeling than a visual, there seems to exist a deeply embedded consciousness, timeless, quiet and profound, weaving of past and present. It is as if some ancient connection informs their daily lives.

We began to wonder if the wisdom they hold, the lives they lead, the cosmology that guides these gentle and hospitable people have relevance for us in the "developed" nations of the world.

What lies under the apparent simplicity? What is their

cosmology? Is it possible or even appropriate to try to understand and adapt in to our own communities and personal lives some of the beliefs that have bound their communities for centuries?

In our quest for answers, several wisdom keepers agreed to be interviewed for a film. This book is a compilation of key points each makes on the topic of ancient wisdom and its application to our modern lives.

SHAMANISM IS AN exclusively western term and it has no analog in cultures which contain the actual experience. This absence of equivalent terms can be explained generally as a result of different world views. Upon encountering something new, the western tradition has tended toward the dissection of the "thing," to separate it, to pull it from its environment and place it under glass or on a wall or in a museum. Or as an entry in a dictionary.

But shamanism does not exist — cannot exist — as a separate entity. We are reminded of the words shared with us by a Peruvian healer now living in the United States: "From the people whose culture contains the experience, shamanism is an integral part of their unfolding.  It is not a separate part of their lives; rather, it is the most vital part.  It is the essential place where they contact the meaningfulness of their lives, as separate individuals, as a community, as one organic whole.  It is what weaves it all together."

To understand and to share our journey from this western culture to their ancient one, we find the use of the word "shamanism" a useful stepping stone for us and for others with whom we share our experiences.  And so we find the need to define it:

> Shamanism is a way of life in which a harmonious relationship between the self, the environment and the spirit world is revealed, attained and maintained.

## *How the Book is Organized*

For clarity and flow, we have organized the information into categories. Even so, the book is not necessarily meant to be read straight through.  We hope you can find on any page a pithy insight, somehow applicable in your own life.

The intent of this book is to serve the discovery of different perspectives, bringing a sense of openness, harmony, wholeness, and contentment into your life.

Most of the statements are cited verbatim.  In some cases we modified and clarified, while maintaining the essence and intent of the comment.

The different colors of text denote statements from the different wisdom keepers we interviewed.

We wish you a grand adventure into new perspectives.

Nancy Wastcoat and Michael Garbett

March 2016

All photography by Nancy Wastcoat

# Wisdom Keepers

Dr. Theo Paredes is a PhD cultural anthropologist who consults with indigenous peoples worldwide to help them preserve their own cultures and communities in the face of advancing research, curiosity, and tourism.

A native of Cusco Peru, Theo has studied Andean healing techniques for more than thirty years, emphasizing the use of sacred plants and native practices for managing energy. He uses his extensive knowledge of the Andean culture to approach ancient sites with a deep understanding of the purposes for which these energetic centers were created. He is the director of the foundation Poqen Kanchay, or "Where Light Germinates." The foundation seeks to rescue, research and teach ancient knowledge and techniques of managing energy to transform living into an art, and to enhance the well-being of all.

**Jose Luis Herrera**, a native of Cusco born into the medicine traditions of the Andes, has spent the last twenty years exploring and studying high Mountain, Amazon, and Coastal medicine traditions of his native Peru.

While formally educated in Civil Engineering and Computer Science, Jose Luis' talents and skills are evidenced in the exquisite beauty and heart he brings to his shamanic teachings.

He's an accomplished mountain climber, explorer, author, speaker, and naturalist. He has studied under the most respected medicine people of Peru and teaches Inka Medicine Traditions across the US and Europe.

**Dr. Armand Bytton** holds a Doctorate of Psychology and Sociology. He has worked with leading experts in business and personal effectiveness. Armand is fluent in English, Spanish and several Amazonian native dialects.

Armand was born and raised in Peru in a family of entrepreneurs. He has maintained a consulting and teaching practice for over 30 years, in which he developed numerous innovative and powerful learning and development programs based on his methodology.

Armand has had life-changing impact on the careers of thousands of clients by allowing his clients to grow into more balanced, successful and happier individuals.

# What is Shamanism?

*Shamanism is the primal ground from which all spiritual traditions have emerged. It is the ancient cosmology of our ancestors who took nature as their spiritual teacher. It has no sacred scripture or dogma. It is a living wisdom, adapted to singular environments and cultures, rediscovered by countless generations who have dared explore hidden landscapes of consciousness and glimpsed the vastness of possibility.*

*Shamanism reminds us of both the fragility and the strength of the web of life, that creation is not a resource to be coerced into fulfilling our insatiable appetites but is a living wonder to be revered and respected. It roots us in our Mother Earth, teaching us its patience, depth, adaptability and incredible power. Nature does not set goals or strive to accumulate.*

*When we become aware of the teachings of Mother Earth, we realize we have enough, we are enough. We see beyond the visible to the spirit worlds. And we realize everything is connected.*

*Shamanism is the bridge between superficiality and the sublime, between fear and the forgotten ways of being. Shamanism shows us the way to reconnect with something timeless and mysterious within the depths of our souls.*

*Influenced by Timothy Freke, Shamanic Wisdomkeepers.*

Shamanism is a way of life integrating and maintaining the deep connection and harmonious relationship of all creation.

Shamanism is not about finding a truth. It is a way of engaging in life and creating an environment for people to discover themselves.

Shamanism is an exclusively western term. From the people whose culture contains the experience, shamanism is an integral part of their unfolding, of their emergence of who they are. It is the place where they are able to contact the meaningfulness of their lives through ritual, through community, and then come back together as one, as a whole. It is what weaves it all together.

Shamanism has been around since people have been on earth. The name comes from the Tungis people in Siberia. It can be translated to mean "he who sees in the dark," or "he

*Shamans are intermediaries between the world of spirit and the world of material. The shaman is an agent who brings balance into the world.*

who works with fire." There are many names meaning the same thing in all parts of the world.

Shamanism has been found in many different countries and has adapted to place, culture, and times, yet maintains its eternal wisdom of life. How this wisdom is portrayed, how it will evolve and the nature of the symbols and rituals will evolve.

*To call it shamanism appeals to a longing for something beyond ourselves, like the father and mother wound in the psyche. That can be dangerous because it delegates responsibilities to something outside ourselves instead of recognizing that responsibility is the ability to respond to one another here.*

Explaining the essence of shamanism is like trying to measure that which is immeasurable; trying to grasp that which is like air. You try to grab it and it disappears; it goes right through your fingers. And yet it is everywhere.

Shamanism comes from a place that is at once constantly evolving and the same. It doesn't follow the rules of linear logic. It is a place we all have, and that we all enter when we go to sleep, the dream time, the place we stumble across when we have very stressful periods in our lives, a place where the rules of logic and the rules of keeping things together fall apart; then there you are. You are in a world that is more intimate than the world of mind, than the world of logic. And yet we have lost touch with the world of meaning, the world of love, the world of wonder, the world of imagination come alive.

Shamanism is not something that is separate from what we do; it's something that is very much a part of what we do. It's what gives meaning to what we do.

Journeying is the core experience of shamanism. Shamanic journey takes you back to a place where you have always been, but you have forgotten: the place of dreams, the place of meaning, and the underlying, under-weaving of everything that is alive.

*Shamans see every day as a gift, an opportunity to grow, an opportunity to find your own light, an opportunity of discovery, an opportunity to come closer to creation itself.*

Shamanism becomes experiencing connectedness, so connectedness becomes a part of us and part of everything we do.

In shamanic societies the beauty and balance of nature has remained intact. We can learn ecologically from the way a tribe lives, from the way that symbols are created to maintain that balance, and thus to embrace ourselves.

# Who are Shamans?
# What Roles Do They Play?

*Shamans act in the capacity of mediators, wisdom keepers, storytellers, teachers, advisors and guides, medicine men and women, soothsayers and sorcerers, driving out evil or heavy energies. They hold together the fabric of their communities, weaving light and balance, harmony and reciprocity.*

*Shamans act as the bridge between the seen and unseen. Through journeying, often with sacred plants, they travel to spirit worlds to retrieve information to heal imbalances in their villagers and villages.*

*Shamans often live at the edge of their communities; when people need them they must go to the edge.*

A shaman is a woman or man who bridges the world of spirit and the world of everyday living. Shamans are able to communicate in both worlds, and bring messages from the spirit world to ease our lives.

Shamans know the world of spirits interpenetrates this reality, and animates the world of objects.

A shaman is a guide in providing an environment for creation and connection to happen. It doesn't matter what language you speak. Creation happens no matter what language you are speaking.

A shaman becomes the vehicle for the awakening of the inner shaman.

A shaman has four job descriptions. One is to ensure fertility ("enka") for all the processes of creation, from the plants we grow in our gardens, our farms, to the well-being of our children, of animals. These traditions are earth-based, agrarian traditions but equally applied to everyday life. Creation is an ongoing process; we are constantly creating great arts of love as well as great disgraces and destruction.

The second job description is "ayni," a Quechua word meaning balance, being in right relationship, creating an environment of harmony. Balance is a term going beyond establishing relationships of power and peace. It has to be a dynamic relationship. That is ayni.

The third job description a shaman has to embrace in taking care of his village is light. Light is the directionality of every aspect of life. Light means if there is darkness, density, or heavy vibration, there needs to be a change through healing and ceremony, changing ideas, building a new vision.

*Shamans help people recognize that they coexist with all creation, and thus discover a deep sense of themselves.*

The fourth job description is wholeness in physical, emotional, spiritual and mental well-being. The primary role of the shaman is to restore balance; to create a framework in which the harmony, the right relationship, the right collective vision can create enough energy for the next change, the next shift, the next project, the next breath to benefit community, individuals, and the land.

Because the shaman has had a very impactful experience of

his own, he is able to have compassion, a sense of connecting, and a sense of intimacy, allowing him to help from a very deep level reestablish a person's integrity within himself.

A shaman is the carrier of the symbolism — the one who stands between the worlds and is able to bridge the two worlds. The shaman brings the symbols into the form of rituals and then helps the people go back and get in touch with themselves, recover dreams, recover what is meaningful.

# Why Shamanism Now?

*Western societies are focused almost solely on consumption and accumulation. We live our lives in a flurry of activities, To Do lists, self- induced obligations. Of course, science and technology have enhanced much in our visible lives, yet at the same time have blinded us to invisible energetic connections that comprise the profound and the sacred.*

*We have extravagance of material and paucity of meaning.*

*We rarely take time to BE, to experience quiet and the rhythmic cycles of life. We rarely sit by a stream or tree or on a mountain top. We are rarely aware of the interconnectedness of all creation... yet this is our source of being and of seeing, of stillness and transcendence.*

*We see ever growing numbers of people yearning and searching for meaning in the midst of mindless activity. More and more of us are opting out of consensual reality and finding our way through Mother Nature and the ancient teachings of modern day Shamans.*

Nowadays people are increasingly distant from nature, and more diseases are occurring. For example, if you take a fish out of water, it might live for five minutes but ultimately it is going to die because you have taken it from its own source of life. What we are doing is taking ourselves out of our own environment, and this is how we are breaking harmony with our environment, our source of life.

*We create imbalance with our actions, with our thoughts, words, because everything is connected with this kamekin [essential source energy].*

The unknown is inside of the known, and we are just beginning to see this unknown. Twenty years ago things like massage, yoga, Reiki, acupuncture, were considered weird and crazy. But now we are beginning to accept that everything is energy and vibrations, and that everything is connected.

There's a sense of separateness, of not being connected, an alienation. The primary complaint is people not knowing how to come together, to heal their souls. The belief we are separate is probably one of the most destructive, violent place we can be, but separateness is our own creation.

Disconnection is a belief that the heart and mind are different, separate. To reconnect we have to realize they are interconnected, to let go of the mind and perceive through the heart. We have the tools to make us feel disconnected. At the core is imagination. What we imagine we become. If we imagine there is disconnection between the heart and mind, that will be what we experience.

*We have gone so far that we believe we own the planet with all the rights to exploit or destroy it...*

In western cultures there is rampant consumerism and lost reverence for the land. The belief is we need to "own." We fill our lives with stuff in an attempt to fill ourselves, yet we have isolated ourselves from the land, and our wholeness is never complete. We have lost our vision and what it means to be human.

Shamans facilitate the feeling of connectedness between the heart and mind. It is not necessary all the time, but to have awareness and choice of a doorway that opens and closes.

In the beginning the challenge for science was to understand what nature was all about. The Newtonian scientists called it "matter" until they discovered that there was no matter. Quantum physicists call it "energy." Beyond this level we will call it vibration or sound.

In the same way we are looking for joy, happiness, health, but our current level of consciousness will not lead us there. We can produce food as never before in human history, but still people are starving, dying of hunger. So there is going to be another shift in the level of consciousness.

The shift is toward a kind of oneness. Ancient wisdom can help make that happen.

Everything seeks balance. The high tech movement is being balanced by a search for spirituality and awareness: organic foods, conservation of nature, health stores, fitness. People are discovering if you lose balance and the harmony, neither technology or science are going to restore the balance... now we are realizing with this kind of attitude we are jeopardizing not only the planet but our own existence.

As in the King Arthur metaphor, many males in western societies are stumbling into the place of having lost their dream, having lost who they are, of having everything material and not having anything. This syndrome is called the Fisher King boy. It is healed by coming together by something that is very instinctual — letting go of the mind, coming back into the body, and realizing that within the body lies an intelligence that is able to heal the psycho-emotional trauma.

People are experiencing a great deal of pain, and do not

know what to do with their pain. They perceive it needs to be fixed instead of relating to it as part of life. They don't have the tools and skills to navigate the terrain.

In our western societies we have lost our sense of self because we have put blinders on, because we don't trust ourselves, we don't trust the fullness of our experience.

Western society has a tendency of relying only on what's observable, on what is tangible, and totally deny the existence of anything else. The measurement by which we lead our lives has the tendency of obscuring what is important.

# Shamanic Cosmology

*Cosmology deals with the origin, development, nature and general structure of the Universe.*

*Shamanic cosmology is based on the concept that everything is alive, everything is in relationship with everything else and everything is infused with Spirit.*

*Also referred to as "Light," Spirit is the source of all life. Shamanic communities acknowledge this and live in conscious communion with all life within their particular environment.*

*Largely detached from their environment Western societies rarely acknowledge their relationship to their environments, causing destruction, desecration and death.*

Shamanic vision is to be aware of the environment in which you live. Cosmic vision literally means how you perceive your environment and the relationship between yourself, your environment and what exists. Each culture has its own logical explanation for understanding that relationship.

Shamanic vision has to do with establishing a synchronous relationship with creation, with light, so light provides you direction, and the relationships become beneficial relationships of power, leading to well-being physically, emotionally, and spiritually.

*Medicine Wheel - Lynn Berryhill*

The Universe is in a state of connectedness, of unity and communion. The cosmology stipulates that every aspect of the Universe is infused with spirits: the land, the rocks, mountains, galaxies. Nothing is absent of spirit.

In this cosmology, there is a way to commune and develop relationships with everything: your workmates, all of nature. This principle, an affinity of power, is "tu-cu-mun-di-neo," loosely translated in Quechua (the language of the Inkas) as the all-encompassing power of unconditional love.

Whenever you are in the space of Tucumundineo

everything is possible; there are no obstacles because spirit is working for your behalf. The Universe is actively conspiring for every pursuit, for every endeavor you are embracing or thinking of creating, that you are stepping into.

The optimal is to find a state of high vibration, such as gratitude, love, compassion, enlightenment, so we can be connected with our creativity, our wholeness, and finding our gifts.

The primordial source of power and membership is connectedness with Pachamama, Mother Earth. Your parents are creators of your physical reality, but the primary connection is with  Pachamama; you are born out of her, you live on her belly, you are nourished from her, and when you die you return to her.

Relationships are very important to the Shaman, and the relationship with Pachamama is absolutely important. People in the West have forgotten the importance of this relationship. They believe everything is separate, disconnected, unrelated. And so the land, air, and water is degraded by corporate greed and for the benefit of a few individuals.

The high mountain shamans know there are mountain beings who are benefactors providing well-being, ensuring crops will be successful. Mountain deities keep the cycles of life in harmony from the rainy season to the dry.

It is important for people in the villages to have relationships with these deities so they do not become predators.

In this view, one of the active parts of training for the shaman is to reclaim his past, so his past, his fears, stories, obstacles, woundedness don't claim the vitality of the individual. Everyday life has to do with being available, being open with an opportunity to regain your wholeness.

There is a concept called Pacha, loosely translated as the allocation of time and space. Time, space, environment, geographic medium, and culture create the perceptions of individuals. Time and space create the culture, the paradigms. But the culture sources out of the generational continuum to find answers to survival, food, shelter.

For example, in the North, you need to have a home with insulation; you need to store food for winter nourishment, and that creates a set of beliefs. In the Amazon, you don't need to store food, as food is in the trees, the fish are in the rivers, and that creates a different belief system.

The land, Pachamama, provides you with an understanding, and the understanding is translated according to your needs. Therefore you create a perception of it. Our perceptions are expressions of Pachamama across generations, across the world. It's really the universe talking to us in different ways.

# Shamanism and Connectedness

*Arguably the most significant difference between modern and indigenous world views is the concept of connectedness. Based on four hundred year old scientific views, western thinking still contains a deeply embedded sense of disconnection and alienation.*

*Beliefs in the separation of body and mind, humans and nature, the sacred and the profane, the environment and the economy, and the belief that humans were "cast from the garden" have led to unimaginable degradation in our relationships, communities, environment, evolution of consciousness, and international relations.*

*The indigenous worldview is that of inextricable interconnectedness of all creation. We all come from the same source, we are all an integral part of nature. The essence of relationship is reciprocity: we have an obligation to grow each other.*

*We are changing. We are becoming more conscious of our impact on the world and on each other. We have the opportunity to explore, understand, validate and embrace the benefits of each worldview, while becoming aware of and eliminating the less beneficial aspects of each.*

The application of this cosmology is to allow individuals, families, villages to begin to take responsibility for their relationships. Shamanic work allows people to regain the power they lost in their stories, family situations, woundedness, causing soul loss or loss of power.

In recovering power, individuals and villages regain balance, and create the vision benefiting individuals and the whole village. The shamanic vision allows the

*It is not necessary to become a shaman or to live within indigenous societies to connect with all creation and to remove incompatible energy around us. We each have innate capacity to manage both internal and external energy.*

individual to empower himself. When he empowers himself he can empower his loved ones, his village.

Even though we have the technology, the internet and web, western culture has the imprint of lone individual, so we haven't been able to fully use the connectedness the web offers. We need to come out from our individual cocoons and use the technology for the benefit of the group.

We need to come back to our clans, our tribes, our villages. With technology we will be able to use our scarce resources more efficiently. It is the idea of the collective. Once the collective in our villages recognizes the need for a vision, we can use our technology to inspire, enhance, and bring together resources to create our vision.

*Connection is a necessary ingredient to being whole. Unity is an experience of connection, aliveness, purity.*

Try to be aware of what we are. We think we are thinking and we are not; we think we are conscious and we are not; we think we are awake and we are not. The first thing is not to try to save the world, it is just to be conscious of your own self.

There is a relationship between an object and a subject. As an example, when I am watching that tree I think that I am aware of that tree. Because all my focus, all my attention is on the tree, I am not aware of my own consciousness, meaning I am the one who is watching the tree. I am focusing on the tree, so I am out of myself. All day long I am my thoughts, outside of consciousness, and so I am not in myself.

The mind is a beautiful tool, but it takes us out of this reality. Mind is always playing between past and future. But those are concepts of space and time. Present is not a concept of space and time. Present is feeling. Present is an experience of what is happening. The first step and the most important for me is to be conscious of what is happening, now in the present.

*The relationship is what makes it work; the relationship is the container for healing. The relationship, the engagement creates the journey to wholeness.*

When the indigenous people of the United States were virtually decimated they became part of the unconscious. So with tribal people there is a constant longing. To tap into a very powerful energy we have to let ourselves sink into the unconscious, and bring it into the foreground.

Right now there is a rediscovery of ritual, storytelling, myth, healing through community (for example we see companies as villages and as living organisms). There will be an adaptation of some of the philosophy and methodology of shamanism in a way that is going to influence inner and outer ecology: the outer ecology of the world and the inner ecology of psychology — the place inside us that needs healing, that needs connection. Shamanism is an important tool for that to happen.

People need to know they are an act of their own self-creation and that involves responsibility.

Responsibility implies connection. One cannot exist without the other.

That also involves freedom. So the first thing to do is recognize the importance of what we do, to value who we are, to value our relationships and our connection to others, and, most important, to value the sacredness of ourselves.

*We all want to belong. Ultimately the world and all society is a tribe. What makes a tribe successful is the belonging to each other.*

There are fundamental experiences we all have, such as the unitive vision, the sense of belonging, the sense of together, the sense of quiet, of peace. All these different basic experiences allow for a sense of ourselves.

Everything talks to me, everything is alive and has significance. What are we connected to? To life, to each other, to everything.

*The shaman's connectedness includes three over lapping elements:*

*Consciousness: Finding one's centeredness to the degree she can connect and remain connected to her Higher Self; maintaining balance between intellect, intuition and instinct; living in a state of gratitude; and remembering*

*Reciprocity: Living in balance; always giving back; maintaining the understanding and practice of continual creation; and right relationship to self, community and the environment.*

*Alignment: Continual maintenance of personal energy; living in harmony with self, others and the universe; living in a state of wholeness and healing; focusing intentions on well-being of self and others; and living in a continual state of contentment.*

# Levels of Engagement

In our travels with different healers we have seen much diversity in the roles they play and the methods they use in their communities.

Cross culturally, however, shamans believe that humans engage with the world through three "centers" within their bodies: intellect (located in the head, the center of thinking), intuition (located within the heart, the center of being), instinct (located within the lower abdomen, the center of doing). These centers must be aligned and balanced in order to live harmoniously within our environment.

A close examination of different cultures reveals the center is most revered within that culture. For example, ancient Greeks revered the intellect above all others. Anglo-Europeans focus on intellect and instinct, enabling the creation of technology to travel to the moon, but ignoring the heart. Indigenous cultures revere the heart connection, creating a sense of connectedness with all creation to the detriment of adopting modern technology.

Realizing they are part of the imbalance evident in the world, in the late 1990s a dozen shamans emerged from their jungles and mountains to meet with North American business leaders and health care professionals. The intent was to engage in a mutual exchange of knowledge (intellect) and wisdom (intuition, unity consciousness).

*Shamans are aware that to maintain their culture and traditions, they must encourage outsiders to gain an appreciation of the richness and depth of the indigenous culture and community. Only through heightened awareness can cultures thrive.*

For the shaman, there are four ways to relate to or engage with situations, themes, information, feelings.

The first is a literal domain or level of engagement.

Something is what it is. I see something, name it, accept it as is. For instance, a traffic light is colored red. That is all — just red, meaning nothing. It is a descriptive conceptualization of something.

The second is the symbolic domain. The traffic light means there is danger. It means I have to stop. It is a symbol for an understanding or an action I take.

The third is the mythic, or metaphoric domain. This is the territory of the ceremony, the ritual in which there is perceptual understanding, not just a conceptual understanding as in the

literal level. In the mythical we see a process or a thing, and we step beyond, bringing ourselves to a place of wholeness, a place of power. In the mythical we recognize the life and the lesson/gift each "time" or event offers us. For instance — back to the red traffic light — we could interpret it as a message to pay attention, to slow down, to consider what we are doing in our life.

For instance: during communion the Christian priest raises a little wafer, a piece of bread (at the literal level) but to him and to believers it is the body of Christ. The cup of wine is the blood of Christ. Can people be healed because they believe the wafer is the body of Christ? Of course.

In the same vein, you can call on the energy of the mountain and you can open your being and welcome the qualities of the mountain, which provides well-being. The mountain is a benefactor of the land. Shamans dwell in that mythical dialogue with nature. In North America there are spirits, power or totem animals serving the same function.

The fourth way of relating is through the essential, the energetic domain. This is pre-verbal engagement, and pure feeling. It is a merging of energy fields — you with the other, becoming the other. There is no thought, no effect. It comes when you are truly in your heart space, truly present.

# Maps of Consciousness

*We in the North subscribe to the myth we were kicked out of the Garden. We believe that we have to work by the sweat of our brow; we have to fight to be accepted; we have to conform; we consume to fill the void.*

*A sense of belonging, connectedness, and of authenticity are of vital importance in our lives. If people are not accepted for who they are through "normal" channels in their communities, they may find more painful and destructive alternatives to being noticed and connected. Thus we see gangs, terrorists, drop-outs, domestic violence, depression, drug abuse, overcrowded prisons, and other symptoms of deeply-seated alienation.*

*What would it be like if we knew each person, regardless of appearance or demeanor, were an integral part of our community, with unique gifts and valuable contributions to the whole?*

*What if we could see behind every behavior a positive intention?*

*What if we adopted an attitude of curiosity, replacing that of judgment, knowing every person is ultimately from the same source? That we are all brothers and sisters.*

*What if we learned that people learn differently, and that it is possible and appropriate to teach and lead to their style, to validate their sense of self?*

> *Could it be so simple that a shift of belief could shift our own maps of consciousness, our world.*

The first maps of consciousness were really star maps. People believed we need to replicate what is written in the heavens, what spirit has given us.

The ruling constellation in the Southern Hemisphere is the Southern Cross, a cluster of four stars. So people lived in a way that community, the village, the family is the absolute denominator of all transactions. The individual comes next.

Though this map is now at an unconscious level, it underpins modern culture in the Southern Hemisphere — the individual sources from the family and from the village, and his obligation is

*The belief we are separate is probably one of the most destructive, violent place we can be... but separateness is our own creation.*

the maintenance of those relationships. In the constitution of earth-based peoples, the idea of the tribe is more important than the individual.

In the Northern Hemisphere, the ruling constellation is the North Star. We live as individuals; the Lone Ranger is our hero living the myth of "rugged individualism." We revere lone hunters like John Wayne going into the sunset by himself.

In the Constitution of the United States the individual is the priority. We have this hero within us, deep in our psyches, going on an epochal journey to make a point, but the hero doesn't take too much responsibility. The hero always ends up alone.

In the North, the myth of origin is that we have been kicked out of the garden. We have fallen from the grace of spirit, and so we need to buy stuff to fill in what is missing.

It is cultural. In the South, the family is essential.

Because they appear to not have much "stuff," we consider them primitive. But they have much more inside: relationships, community, support.

One of the most interesting things I witnessed the first time I came to North America is the absence of plazas. In Latin America we have plazas, and on Sundays or evenings people gather, sit on the benches, talk about anything and everything that is happening in their homes, jobs, lives. Here in North America we go to malls or sit at home watching TV.

# What is Energy?

*Energy can be described as vibrating fields of waves and particles. Waves are invisible patterns with no fixed position in space or time. Particles are substantive and visible patterns, manifested forms. While everything exists simultaneously in both states, the "state" of energy depends on the focus of our attention.*

*We experience the forces of energy in our daily lives, not only with our cell phones, television, satellites, X-rays, MRIs and other technology, but also through forces such as gravity, emotions, thoughts, feelings, relationships and cultures.*

*For thousands of years, wisdom keepers in every culture have realized that creation, the shift from wave to particle state, occurs through the effects of intention and attention, or observation. In other words, we create both our experiences and actual material things through those actions.*

*The following excerpts describe how modern wisdom keepers describe this force.*

There are many ways to understand energy. We call energy "kamekin," something that allows things to exist. It is best experienced through feeling, not thinking. It is alive, a permanent shifting transformation that is existence itself. Now we are gaining from science a better understanding of these refined qualities in electromagnetic fields and vibrations we generate.

We are created from this kamekin. We are a part of everything. There is kamekin in you and me, in the tree, in the cloud. So we all come from the same source; we are all equals, we are all brothers. We all depend on each other.

*Everything talks to me, everything is alive and has significance.*

If you make any damage to any part you are making damage to yourself, and you are able to feel it. So I cannot make damage to the planet because I am damaging myself. This is the shamanic way of seeing nature.

We are the world. We are the planet. So what we do to ourselves we do to the planet. Ecology is everything, including ourselves. We are part of mother earth; we are mother earth. So to the extent we take care of ourselves we take care of the planet, and vice-versa.

Energy is the vital force, the chi, essence of life, that moves and is a part of everything. What makes us alive is not all our organs doing their thing, but the vital energy moving inside us. Energy is the fuel of life, the key ingredient.

*Life is about dialogue, a sharing and exchange of energy.*

Shamans use their own vital energy to help people get in touch with their energy so they can feel their aliveness.

While some people can see energy, most of us can feel it when we pay attention. So instead of comparing selves with others who see energy, we can facilitate people to FEEL energy and discover that emotions are an expression of energy.

From emotions the seeing comes. It is seeing with the body, a presence of the body and the availability of the body through the movement of all energy and the energy of life.

What's interesting is people are looking for something tangible when they themselves are not tangible. Ask a person, "Who are you and where are you? I'm not going to talk to you until you show me who you are." What, are they their body? No, they're many many more things and all these different things coming together — that's energy; that's the expression of energy through an individual.

Energy can be defined as opposite and complementary forces coming together, and becoming one, and then out of that oneness, that unity. This is the basic principle of life.

Everything is one and everything is many.

Western culture lives in a philosophy designed for one person. Thus, it excludes dialogue, and in excluding dialogue it excludes life. Because life is about dialogue, and exchange and sharing of energy. What is energy? A dialogue.

# What is Fear?

As is everything, emotions are patterns of energy. Any emotion creates an instantaneous physical response in our body and within our field of energy, and is therefore detectable by anyone and anything in our immediate environment.

For instance, within two seconds of one moment of anger, every space of our body is flooded with the hormones associated with that emotion. More significantly, five hours later our immune system is still suppressed.

Habitual patterns of low frequency emotions create imprints in our energy field and can eventually cause dis-ease in our body.

If, as research indicates, everything is interconnected, our emotions also affect our world and the universe. It behooves us, therefore, to attend to our emotions, to manage our energy.

How do we do this? By becoming aware of what we are feeling and thinking, and noticing how that feels in our body. Our body has wisdom, and gives us constant signals as to yes/no, right/wrong, effective/ineffective.

When we know our selves as being of light, as an integral aspect of nature, there is nothing to fear.

Fear is not the enemy. Fear is one of the ways that the body talks to us. But when the body talks to us in fear it is letting us know we are not loving ourselves. So fear is not the problem; not loving ourselves

*Human technology excludes nature, and thus we are destroying ourselves through technology because we are part of nature.*

is. Don't try to get rid of fear; instead let me love myself, and in doing that we establish balance.

The purpose of fear is to create boundaries. The primary expression of fear is to create safety. Safety always involves boundaries. It always involves exclusion of something.

So what needs to happen is the re-establishment of the balance between fear and self-love. There is fear because there is a lack of connection with each other.

How can you be afraid when you are connected? How can you be afraid when the world is whole?

# What is Healing?

The Word "to Heal" comes in part from the Greek root, "eu" meaning "well."

From this root we also get eulogy (to speak well of), euphoria, euphemism (to speak fair), eucharist (to give thanks, show favor, give freely), eupeptic (having good digestion). We also get health, holy, wholeness, beneficial, and many other modern terms.

Healing, therefore, implies wholeness, perhaps holiness. Being whole can be considered a sacred state of being.

Wholeness also implies authenticity (we are the authors of our own lives), and a recognition of the essential balance of light and dark within a person. A person is neither all light nor all darkness, but a blend of both. To be whole presumes this awareness, so that moderating forces can be brought to bear on any situation.

A primary role of shamans is to heal, to rebalance energy. They understand illness as an imbalance in the energy field. Imbalance is always evident at the least dense, intangible level before it shows up physically within a person's body, the most dense level.

Because shamans are able to perceive the imbalance, they can remove incompatible energy forms from a person's or community's energy field through a variety of timeless processes and techniques.

*On the other hand, conventional western medicine focuses on curing physical and tangible symptoms. Because the physical level is templated on the least dense, invisible, intangible level, curing only physical symptoms results in reversion to the imbalanced state. Thus we see multiple back surgeries, cancer surgeries, heart surgeries.*

Healing, becoming whole, can only happen through a sacred experience. To heal from any malady, the most important step is to stop the mind from constructing what should be. It is only what "is" that can heal. What "should be" can never be healed. Why? Because it is not real. Creating an experience of self is creating an experience of what is, including the confusion.

*Shamanic tools are experiences allowing a true dialogue to emerge. Much of the dialogue is non-verbal; we can talk with our beingness. The most important conversations often take place not in what is being said but in how we are creating space together.*

Confusion is just a part of clarity. We would not be confused unless we wanted clarity, so the two are together.

To create an experience of being yourself, feel the desire to be yourself and let the longing guide you. Trust the feeling and the feeling will take you where you belong. Stop numbing yourself. Feel the pain of the moment, feel the kiss of your own grief, the grieving for the self that has been lost.

Losing paradise is losing ourselves. Losing connection with life, connection with what is here, what is real. That's the sense of loss, the sense of confusion, of not quite knowing how to go back to the garden, not realizing that the garden is right here, present.

So the first step is to feel the pain, and not trying to get rid of it. Surrender what is, to what is inside you. Be available to yourself. Be vulnerable to yourself. Surrender to your dreams and dare to fulfill them.

Second, be vulnerable to what life brings you. Take the journey, because your pain will be the most important guide you have. Usually as we experience pain there will be a place where something from inside of us will come forward and say, "Hey, remember your dreams." The journey is a journey of remembering and of putting yourself back together.

That is what lies at the core of the mystery. Because it is more an unconscious act, more an invitation and a surrender. It is through surrender that we begin to remember.

The first tool is to let go. How do we recognize that we can let go? By recognizing that we are holding on. And what we are holding onto is the ephemeral, something not even real. The second tool is choice. The third is courage to step into the choices as fully as possible and make them happen.

Some people are in a constant state of surrender, and they need to do the opposite: they need to know where to stand, and grab hold of something. Everyone is along the continuum of surrender to making a stance. It's knowing where you are and knowing the next step: surrender or hold on to regain one's self.

Shamanic tools are experiences allowing a true dialogue to emerge. Much of the dialogue is non-verbal; we can talk with our beingness. The most important conversations often take place not in what is being said but in how we are creating space together.

We still carry the load of our younger years as pains in our back. If we could take our collective history, place it in the fire, and release it, we would ensure a wonderful future for our children.

It is necessary for us to craft a new vision though bringing out the qualities of the heart, of compassion, and understanding the importance of the land, the village and the collective.

It is not about becoming a shaman; it is about regaining wholeness and being driven by a vision that will benefit yourself and the people around you, because ultimately we source from people around us: from our parents, our community, our children. Our responsibility is to have

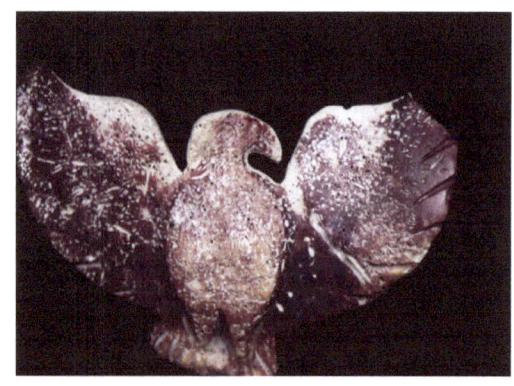

*Shamans heal by changing the energy, creating a higher vibration.*

a relationship of balance with them. As you walk into the next day, the next season, the relationship needs to be driven by a vision.

Healing is not about fixing. Healing has to do with a

process of embodiment of belief systems. Once you have that core belief system as your map, then you can bring the necessary energy to produce the change and the healing. Healing is holistic. It has to do with bringing wholeness into the different areas of a person's life, in relationship to what he does, to his family, to his dreams.

A person must find balance, must be able to heal himself, and to be claimed by life and power rather than his hurts, his stories, his wounds.

The first step is to practice compassion for yourself, to be more aware of what is driving your vehicle, your life. Once there is compassion, there is the opportunity for your blinders to come off; then you can heal.

In situations where people are in destructive behavior that is hurting them and serving them at the same time, or have a behavior they are hanging on to and don't know how to let it go, you have to provide an experience to help them want to change.

Many don't see a need to change, because they believe they have everything: money, big homes, material stuff, but they are empty inside; they have struggling relationships, are not happy. The easiest and fastest route is to create an experience that is equally as irrefutable.

Every experience has its opposite. For example, a person wants to die, but within them is a place that doesn't want to die, a living force. So the shaman stalks that living force, (meaning to bring forth what is not seen; to bring light to the darkness; to bring to the foreground what is in the background), and creates a kind of mirror of the life force, and then lets the opposites exist in relationship. The opposites themselves will begin to generate another place where they can come together (mediating internal differences). It is like having a thesis, and antitheses and synthesis, and a container or space to play in — all of which make up the four elements of any situation.

So a person brings the shaman a thesis, a place where he stands. The shaman needs to generate the experience of the antithesis. The creation of the polarity causes a momentum and generates a creative flow that allows the antithesis to be embodied in the person, as it brings to the foreground the doubts, the confusion, the places where the person begins to recognize he wants something more. And when you want something more, you become more available to more of yourself.

People get this experience through a simple exercise of asking questions: Are you in a place where you are the most happy? Are you really happy with your life? Do you live in the way you want to live? Are you caring in the way you would like to be caring?

If you stop to feel where you are and to ask yourself that

question, and answer "no," the shaman has to ask, "What are you doing? You know life is short, right? So live." When you bring these questions to light, and feel the pain, the encounter of the self can help reveal the self to the self.

The problem with the practice of psychology is that there is always something to be fixed. There is always something not quite right, and therefore you are broken and need to be fixed. The experience of the creative process involving shamanism is not that you need to be fixed. It's that you are constantly creating.

So let us give you the choice to create in the direction most aligned with your own spirit's longing. From the experience of the self everything unfolds.

# Creating Reality

*Quantum physicists support what shamans have known for thousands of years: we literally create our own realities.*

*For example: imagine building, say, a birdhouse or a business (or anything else). First, you have the belief that it is possible. Then you imagine it in more detail, draw up plans, and gather the resources needed to achieve what you have visioned in your imagination.*

*Manifestation originates with intention, which creates a criteria-bounded channel through which your energy flows, followed by attention, which focuses and attracts the necessary resources.*

*Our beliefs cause energy fields that in turn create our realities. What we believe is what we see.*

*It is said that everything already exists in pure potential. Our part is to receive what is there, then express gratitude for having the chance to choose.*

*In other words, whatever you seek, also seeks you through the concept of "affinities" or relationships.*

How can we change our reality? We can become aware of and redefine our myths and our stories and rituals. Become more conscious of them, so we can create a sense of self that is more available to ourselves

The patterns will always exist, so it is not a matter of eliminating patterns. Having a sense of self will allow us to choose the patterns we want to express ourselves through. That is the most important.

Our perception patterns, our beliefs are rituals. They continue to unfold even when we are not conscious of them.

We are constantly creating — that is something we cannot avoid. We are constantly generating ourselves, we are constantly creating each other and relationship to each other. I am not saying we create the tree or this chair, and yet somebody else must have been involved in doing it.

What I am saying is that we create our interaction, our

relationship, how we feel about the tree, the chair, each other. What we create are the conditions that allow for our interactions to be real. Within that feeling, we have a choice.

Most people would choose to be happy, for example, yet most people are miserable. Why is that? Because they are always seeking for someone else to help them out instead of realizing their inner shaman, that they have everything that is available to help themselves be happy. It takes courage to create it.

The strongest perpetrator is the victim. It takes a great deal of energy to be a victim and to remain there. Imagine what would happen if that energy were used for the opposite; instead of "life is doing all this to me," to engaging life and creating from life and creating with life. The most important is the experience of self.

# Evolving Consciousness

*How we evolve our consciousness defies an easy answer, as it means we have to define consciousness, a central topic of nearly all religions for millennia. Of the hundreds of practices promoted for evolving consciousness included are meditation, yoga, vision quest, prayer, pilgrimage, sun dance, body work, silent retreat, fasting, living authentically and purposefully.*

*But what is consciousness, and why do we need to "evolve" it?*

*We offer a possibility: consciousness may be considered a vibratory pattern of energy that in-forms our lives. It is eternal, inextricably interconnected with all creation, and holographic in nature, meaning that each person's consciousness is an aspect of cosmic consciousness.*

*Evolution of consciousness then, could mean raising the frequency of the vibration, enabling us to access higher levels of awareness, connectedness, power and perspective, thus easing our lives and the lives of others with whom we come in contact.*

## How can we evolve consciousness?

Two to four million people a day visit psychologists and psychiatrists in this country. It means that money doesn't make you happy, money doesn't give you peace, money doesn't give you harmony, money does not even buy you health. Evolving levels of consciousness become paths to fulfillment, satisfaction, and to moving beyond the material.

*When you become aware, conscious, you become that which are you are conscious of. Whatever you focus on, that you will be. Whatever is deep in your heart, that is who you are. Consciousness allows us to become who we really are.*

Individual consciousness is a contribution to the cosmic consciousness, and we are not using the consciousness yet in the right way.

Our concept of time is not linear, does not go from past, present to future. Our concept is cycles: something begins, something ends. The cycle of earth, the "biological clock" is beginning to ring. We have had to go through wars, violence, fighting, to reach other levels. Now the young children are beginning to feel the planet in another way. It has nothing to do with their religion. They are beings of high levels of consciousness.

The greatest gift a person can give himself is the autonomy

of his consciousness as he passes into the next world. To have been able to live life to the fullest, to have been able to have embodied presence and left a legacy of power, of love to your people.

If that is the case, then consciousness evolves and when you die they say your consciousness comes with you, and your physical reality goes back to the land. The legacy of power stays with your people, but your consciousness evolves, merges with larger organizing principles, and you return to the stars.

On a day to day basis, higher levels of consciousness allows you to see 360. Higher levels allow you to step beyond your personal needs, to accomplish a self-realization process and to find your purpose: what are you here for, what are your responsibilities. Our responsibility is to our village and to a stewardship to this wonderful vessel of nutrients, of gifts we call Mother Earth.

An altered state is tapping into a place that we normally don't live from, that allows us to acquire a different way of relating to ourselves. Examples of typical altered states are dreaming, driving a car, watching TV, daydreaming, meditating. We all engage in these states without even being conscious of what we are doing.

## What does it mean to walk the beauty way?

Walking the beauty way means embracing all of ourselves. It is the sense that it is okay to be myself. It feels like being in love all the time. Instead we are constantly judging ourselves and not realizing our own beauty.

## What is meant by "between the worlds"?

In between the tangible and intangible, observable and unobservable, audible and inaudible. The separation of these worlds is a western construct.

## How do people in western societies realize they are touching another world?

When they listen to a beautiful song, and are carried back by the song, and a little part of them is healed: that is a shamanic moment.

## How can we deliberately walk between the worlds and bring the two worlds together?

Bring aesthetics, the beauty of life into consciousness. Cultivate the sanctity and sacredness of daily life. The essential task is to live our lives from the place that is most meaningful. It's not something we have to do; it's something we have to embrace and allow to be expressed.

# Religion and Shamanism

*The word religion originates from Latin "ligo," "ligare," meaning to tie, to bind, to connect, as in ligament. "Re-ligio" then is to re- connect.*

*Indigenous cultures have no concept of disconnection; they live in the garden, having never left. They would not understand the need to reconnect. These cultures are intimately bound to the land, Pacha Mama, Mother Earth, for whom they express and live in constant gratitude – not just on one day a week.*

*They realize they ARE Earth, they ARE Spirit, known by thousands of names. There is no separation. They see no need for an external intermediary, doctrine, or dogma to teach them the "rules" of connectedness and honoring the Source of Life.*

*Their lives are founded on both conscious and unconscious forces that connect them to all creation. Thus they communicate – create community – with deep knowingness of the interdependence of all creation.*

## What is the difference between religion and shamanism?

Shamanism is not a religion. Religion has dogma theology. Religions promote separation and duality. There is God, out there, and there is you. There is a gap, and you need to go through repentance, hardship, salvation and have intermediaries to get closer to God. How about finding God inside, having direct access?

Shamanism is a way of being, a way of relating to yourself and to the Universe. Shamans believe there is no intermediary between you and the Great Mystery, between you and God. You go and talk to God directly.

Something I find quite amusing in formalized religions is that we are encouraged to pray to God, and when God talks back to us, we are called schizophrenic.

Religion is a set of dogmas, a set of practices enforced by a priest, who becomes a vehicle for the rules and policies, enforcing a belief system.

Shamanism is about inviting you to experience where the belief system comes from. A priest teaches you about truth; a shaman takes you into the truth. A priest talks about God, and the feeling of God. A shaman says, "Come, let's play with the Gods." It's a very direct experience of the sacred.

Let me give an example. Many people practice yoga, which is a way to help grow your physical body, your consciousness, your breathing, your way of eating. So I could be Buddhist and practice yoga; I could be Christian and practice, I could be Jewish and practice yoga. Because it is something that deals with my everyday life.

Religion in the beginning was something like yoga, something that teaches people to keep harmony in their own environment, with family, with society. But when religions become institutionalized they started to fight with each other as to who is the keeper of the real truth: "my God is the real god, and your God is evil."

Religions always create morals. Morals are not the same for all religions: Hindus have morals, Christians have other morals, Judaism has other morals. So which moral is the real one? The result is that religion becomes something like a social club.

In shamanism you reach a level of consciousness wherein you act knowing what is good and what is bad, but not because a tradition tells you to do this or do that.

The main difference between religion and shamanism is that shamanism is the most pure, pristine level of consciousness without any rules or prejudices against any other.

# Spirituality and Shamanism

*What is the difference between religion and spirituality?*

*As we noted earlier, religion can be translated as "reconnection." The path through which every current religion has evolved is an alleged connection to the Source, called by a thousand names, through a complicated system of filters. These filters usually come in the form of often self-anointed, male figures who create dogma, specific buildings used exclusively for worship that can only take place there, hierarchical lists of "thou shalt" and "thou shall nots" and often extremely differing rules for men and for women.*

*Spirituality is direct access to the Source.*

*No intermediaries required. Available to all. Available anywhere. All free to interpret their experiences as they choose. No right and wrong, good or bad, angelic or satanic.*

*Just like shamanism.*

*"The teaching of the Tao Te Ching is moral in the deepest sense. Unencumbered by any concept of sin, the Master doesn't see evil as a force to resist, but simply as an opaqueness, a state of self-absorption which is in disharmony with the universal process, so that, as with a dirty window, the light can't shine through.*

*When people see some things as beautiful, other things become ugly. When people see some things as good, other things become bad.*

*Being and non-being support each other. Difficult and easy support each other. Long and short define each other. Before and after follow each other."*

*From Tao Te Ching, translated by Stephen Mitchell*

Spirituality is a sense of connectedness through the sacredness of life. Connecting with people in a way that respects the integrity of a person's expression: an experience of the web of life, the experience that we are all connected, we are all one, we are all each others' best friend.

## *What is God?*

God spirit in this cosmology is creation itself. The different expressions of creations are found in your babies, in the knowledge that there is nothing that is evil, for evil is a western conception. Evil or darkness or negativity is just an aspect of low vibration.

*Note: Look at the spelling of "Evil" Turn it around and it becomes "Live". Evil may be considered "living backwards," living outside the Law of Origin, the Laws of Nature.*

*Do the same with "Devil".*

# Business and Shamanism

*Many of us seem to have lost sight of the original purpose of business, so we go back to a root meaning. In Old Swedish, "business" means "nourishment for life." Current Swedish translates "company" to "break bread together." (Com = with, Pane = bread). We forget that "organization" is derived from "organic," "organ," "organism" all pointing to "wholeness." And that "corporation" derives from "corpus" or "cell."*

*Shamanic leaders see the whole and are able to tell the story that is alive but invisible within the culture. They are able to weave and walk into the next dream. They have 360 degree perspective: hindsight, foresight, insight, oversight and peripheral vision — they see from a higher perspective and the higher design. They look to the impact on the 7th generation rather than to short term gains.*

*They operate selflessly from ethics — the firm and free line for the good of all; being in the flow, separating doing for oneself to doing for others. They operate from organic principles — working together to make the organism whole and complete, and the corpus to thrive, knowing each cell is of vital importance.*

*Shamanic leaders have a different concept of competition: rather than "winner takes all," they understand there are four distinct aspects of competition: the confrontation (meeting), the contest, the collaboration, the celebration ("Raymi"). The person who "wins the race" has a moral obligation to teach others how she won, so the community grows as a whole, rather than individuals accumulating knowledge and talent.*

*The key attribute of shamanic leaders is "Ayni," meaning reciprocity and harmony. If there is no Ayni in their organization, the life force is diminished and the organism withers. Ayni is the "law of origin," the flowing interconnectedness of all creation.*

Business is an interchange of services. Business is like breathing; I have to breathe out before I can breathe in again; I have to give before I receive. It is the movement of energy: giving and taking, giving and taking.

*We can see corporations as villages, where everyone is important, and everything is integrated.*

We have misunderstood the point that in giving so much value to money, which we relate to power and control, we are forgetting to create services. Controlling and repressing others, making someone do something against his will, creates instability, leading to corrupted societies.

We have lost the idea of play, of joy for its own sake, so much so that all our activities, play and work, have become competitions.

Go into business with the intention of good and joy, for the fun of it. Business is an art. You will enjoy it more than if you fight it. You can become successful in this way for yourself, for your business, and for others, teaching them how to create a better quality of life.

## How do shamans work with corporations?

We can see corporations as villages. Energy in villages flows because the villagers think and feel as a body where each part of the body is important. For example, if I am the manager I am the head, and you are the doorman, the little toe. But if you cut the little toe, the manager cannot walk, and there is pain to the whole body. Each part has to be integrated. Everyone has his or her own role, own space, but it doesn't mean that one part is more important than another.

First you need to tap into the energy of an organization. What is the energy that organizes that reality? What are the affinities found there? What is the purpose? What is the vision, and how does it benefit the corporation, the stockholders? What are the responsibilities of the board members? Does the vision/purpose only benefit the stockholders and executives or does it also benefit the land, the employees, the community?

The shaman goes into an institution, understands the energy; and if there are affinities that do not provide wholeness, those need to be healed. So the shaman brings wholeness, and sets the affinities to create the next dream, the next project.

In working with either an individual or a corporation the

essential act is to guide a person to open his heart, to see what is absolutely important to that individual. Is it money, is it happiness?

Once we have found what is important, we discover the roots: where did it come from? Parents, bosses, teachers? Then we create balance in work, family relationships and environment that is supportive. From that base we can create a product that will benefit the public, the shareholders, the employees.

# Government and Shamanism

*Consider this:*

*We believe the "government" is "the other." It is over there. It is them. It is not us: we are the good guys, it is the bad guys.*

*We forget that the government is us. We willingly elected our peers to serve. Then we vilify and condemn. We placed high hopes on them and their promises that they would solve each of our problems, create each of our ideal visions for our country. We forget or cannot imagine the forces playing in the field to which our elected friends are now subject.*

*Could it be that the government is a shadow of ourselves? Is it possible that the government reflects back to us that which we cannot see in ourselves? Perhaps it is easier to condemn in others what we condone in ourselves. Perhaps we have been taught that we are separate and disconnected from each other. When we bemoan the idea that the "government" has no vision, no sense of deeper purpose, are we really casting our unknown, unrecognized self onto "it?"*

*Something to think about at least, even if it may not be true.*

We are our government in many ways, because the government mirrors our own doubts and our own confusion. To the extent we are whole, the government will be whole.

The essential task for this country is the rediscovery and recovery of soul. The United States is very fragmented and has lost its purpose. It is a place where the world is new and where many can become one. There is a possibility of learning how to live together.

*Embodying the work of the shaman means to take stewardship, to take care, to provide and bring balance. Anyone who is dedicated to the preservation of the land, working in the healing and spiritual roles, bringing people back to normalcy and wholeness are shamans for their communities.*

The United States is very young, yet the people are living on top of an ancient world that has barely been allowed to live (the North American tribes). The people are desperately seeking themselves with very few tools to do that. There is a deep desire to connect with something that is sacred, meaningful. That is difficult to do because the tools and the skills of navigating what is not tangible are not available.

I have two images of the United States: one is this big advance in technology, and the other is an evolving mind and consciousness, and returning to respect this planet that we are a part of. They are coming into balance.

# Shamanism and Modern Culture

*We have the concept that shamans live far away and long ago in villages deep in jungles, deserts, and forgotten islands. Yet if we recognize that the roles shamans play in their communities include healing, leading, balancing energy, story telling, ritual making, mediating, bringing new insights, discovering and recovering souls (among many others), then is it not also realistic to see many many shamans in our own neighborhoods?*

*Modern shamans, dressed not in feathers and furs, but disguised in suits and sweats and jeans, may come in the form of leaders, healers, teachers, painters, writers, poets, filmmakers, medicine people, gardeners, builders, sport coaches, consultants, pilots, visionaries, explorers, photographers. Anyone who takes us out of consensual reality to journey to other worlds, to see other possibilities, is a shaman.*

*Look around and you may recognize your fellow shaman from the light in her eyes, the glow of his persona, the kind and caring interaction with others.*

*Look inside. Maybe you are a shaman too, balancing energy, bringing harmony and reciprocity, being present, healing others just by being the "you" you were meant to be.*

*Aren't we lucky?*

Shamans have many roles in modern societies, but they don't have titles. Authors, artists, actors and actresses, filmmakers, healers, musicians, pioneers, poets, politicians, scientists... those who create environments where people discover themselves, to discover their own I-am-ness. Based on the sense of I-am-ness, people are able to embrace their suffering, their joy, the fullness of their humanity.

*Shamans teach us about regaining wholeness and being driven by a vision that will benefit yourself and the people around you...*

Shamans haunt and hunt for images to help people unfold, focusing consciously to bring forth the essence of what it means to be alive, to bring the perennial stories, the things that lie at the core of who we are as human beings.

For example, movie making is a form of shamanism. It is an expression of ritual. You go to a movie, sit down, are impacted by the images, and then journey with the images. That is a form of shamanism... a shamanic practice.

# Shaman's Messages to the World

A great cosmological shift is happening. We see evidence all around us. What is going on?

There is more attention to the environment, renewable power, sustainability, organic food, social justice, energy healing and shamanic experiences, natural medicine, higher levels of consciousness in businesses.

Shamans are gathering in many parts of the world including Alaska, Europe, Africa, South America, Asia to hold a vision and the space for the planet's becoming. Recently, the Dalai Lama spent 30 days mediating on an island in Lake Titicaca, anchoring the transfer of planetary energy from the Himalayas to the Andes.

These remarkable people are recognizing the importance of sharing their age-old wisdom with the awakening "younger brothers and sisters" in the developed world.

We acknowledge with gratitude and love the efforts on the part of so many we have worked with.

Here are some of their messages:

# *If you could give a message to the world, what would it be?*

Since we were young we were taught to see outside ourselves. Now is the time to start to see inside — to see our own selves.

*More than the learning is the remembering. We have to remember what we are, where we have come from, why we are here...*

We don't need external teachers or masters. They will teach you their way. Everything is inside us and if we look deeper into these levels of consciousness we are going to find our own teachers, our own guides who will help us live our life as we should.

## Stop. Feel. Dream.

Stop: take a pause; don't rush; consider. Let that become part of everyday.

Feel: really allow yourself to sink into yourself.

Dream: dream what is most real, most meaningful for you. Let that be the place you contact inside yourself.

And enjoy your life. Enjoy what you create; enjoy your family and the simple things because the extraordinary is always grounded in the ordinary. The sacred and the profane sleep with each other. Enjoy the dream; come and journey with us.

## Be still. Connect with spirit. Express gratitude.

Assemble your reality so you do not collude with the consensual, the pre-programmed reality based on yesterday and tomorrow. What happened yesterday spills into today and you will be part of that traffic.

Practice reverence: find a place within you that is not held hostage by your fears, insecurities, memories; a place of balance. Find a way to talk with, connect with, dialogue with your higher self.

Be still. Find a way, perhaps meditation, to practice stillness. Come into one's self, move away from chatter.

Practice gratitude. Prayer (dialogue with higher self), stillness, gratitude allows you to come into wholeness. Then you can walk into the traffic of everyday and you are not going to be colluding with the consensual. You will perceive differently, with awareness, you will see a larger view metaphorically and keep things in perspective. Any fears, insecurities, other thoughts and emotions may still be with you, sitting in your lap, but will not be part of any transaction you have with others or with the environment. These practices will provide you with a better opportunity to see what the day has to offer. You will be more available; you will be able to see clearly all the options in a decision; you will practice presence. You will be more observant, more practical, heal faster, and make changes more readily. Spirit/God is more available to us, and we can invite it to us. We need to take responsibility and not blame our troubles on God. Live the fullest with reverence, have respect for our children, our resources, the earth, our actions, our responsibilities. Exercise full presence.

## How you are contributing to community?

Our friend Rick related these messages from his experience at Burning Man:

From your own sense of authenticity, choose your own adventure among the millions of options. It is possible to move at will in and out of various adventures.

Be present. This life is your choice... live it fully.

Be generous. We are meant to grow and evolve together from everyone and everything. Remember the concepts of reciprocity, ayni.

The Burning Man experience is meant to be a microcosm of the universe... To be what you want. How you want. When you want.

### Be light. Be life. Be love.

Express gratitude for everything, and everything you want will come. When we become light there is no room for dark. When we acknowledge our brilliance there is no room for self-doubt or denigration, "not good enough" or fear.

## Disclose each other. Create a collective mesa. Grow old together.

*We each have a star of wholeness within us. We each have an obligation to change the dense energy around us. We must connect with the energy that creates everything.* - Dona Maria

# Interested in buying more books for yourself or others?

Buy online directly from Lulu at

http://www.lulu.com/spotlight/WiseGuides

OR

Contact us by email at nancy@wiseguides.us

(You may request an autographed copy.)

**Spanish version coming soon!**

www.ingramcontent.com/pod-product-compliance
Lightning Source LLC
Chambersburg PA
CBHW040457240426
43665CB00038B/15